PRAISE F

BAREFOOT AND RUNNING

"Morgan Liphart's *Barefoot and Running* blends the topographies of place and heart to reach a fitful communion between them. At once lyrical and candid, these poems sojourn 'across the border of ourselves' into fresh realms of inner and outer weather. While this shared space may be tinged with regret, it is also elevated by the outstretched hand of possibility — the poet's notion that indeed there are "stars inside your bones" at any altitude."
— Kevin Stein, author of *American Ghost Roses* and Illinois Poet Laureate 2003-2017

"In Morgan Liphart's work we encounter more than a distinct voice, we encounter a writer willing to be vulnerable, a writer of heart and intelligence. Even through the fog of grief Liphart bravely delivers the good news 'Hope is not a dead language / it whispers in our sleep.' In this collection of poems I believe it not only whispers but calls each and every one of us by name."
— Matthew Dickman, author of *All American Poem* and Guggenheim Fellow

Barefoot and Running

Morgan Liphart

Cover design by Robyn Bieber with Seventh & Gray.
Author photograph by Bernadette Uzcategui with Blueprint
Society.

ISBN: 978-1-7359579-0-6

Acknowledgements to the editors and staff of *Off the Coast*
(Barefoot and Running), *Third Wednesday* (Smooth), and
The Docket (Part I: Leaving, Part II: Arriving) for publishing
versions of poems that appear in this chapbook.

For every woman who has felt like not enough.
My darling, you are so much more than enough.

Contents

This is where I leave you.

Part I: Leaving

The wrinkled map I keep in my trunk
is set and smoothed on the dashboard with shaking palms.
My sister may worry. Missed calls,
spare apartment keys turning to find empty.
My finger traces Colorado. I move west
through blank cornfield roads,
then mountains and forest. Stiff limbs locked up, silent,
living out of my jeep with the rims bent in.
When I wake each morning, fog clouds
the windshield like a memory I push to the edge
of myself, details melting away.
I speed through smoky towns,
past every dirty gas station across the state line —
the line between me and my inherited sadness,
as if I could cross that border in myself too.
I leave behind the silent defeats of my mother
and her mother and her mother before her,
raising children in a farmhouse, youth crumbling
like soil in the field. It's enough just to try to run.
My toes push the pedal down while my cell chokes in mud
on the bottom of the Rock River.
I used to hold on with white knuckle fists, now
the ashes of my life are light on the wind
and my palms empty. West. I drive west,
watching yellow blinking lines on the pavement
blur together, like a hum of prayers
for second chances. And hope combusts
in my fuel tank,
                    .the most powerful force that exists.

Part II: Arriving

I am standing in a field in Breckenridge, wondering
if a soulmate can be a place, instead of a person.
My hair blurs into the gold, wild grasses of fall
until there is no separating me from the land,
the land from me. This is how it was always
meant to be. I can roll my ear to the earth
and hear her welcome me home. I'm just sorry
it took me so long.

At the top of bluebell trail, underneath a douglas fir

In the wind, in the rocks
with the bones of fine dust
I'm burying you eight years too late
It took that long to leave
the sticky town we grew up in —
        as if the tangled roots of it wouldn't give us up

Its breath crackled and its buildings shook
with the weight of your grief,
then the weight of my grief   after
they found you in the garage with a rope,
        finally lighter than air

No school assembly was held for you
No signs or ribbons coated the town
    There is only me, only you
 and our one set of footsteps on a sandstone path,
 deciding that if you didn't feel the freedom
 of the sharp scent of pine and a borderless map
        in life, then   maybe   freedom in death
            is the next best thing

Fragments of earth cover
my hair and cheeks like soot
    as I scoop you out from the core
with my hands cupped like spades

        All I can do
    is give you a new home
I can carry the weight of both of us,
    your ashes and my apologetic body,
to the misted top of mountains
you'll never get to see

So let your second life
    your softer life be
        not somewhere else
           but here

           Then, here,   a bluebird sings

To Adam, From Eve

I eat 18 apples.
One for every time I want to call your name
but close my mouth instead.
This is how I learn the slow rot of loss.
This is how we become a lesson pressed
between gilded pages.

In hell, there are seven rooms.

In this room, you kiss me once
    and never again.

In this room, there are a hundred paper horses.
    Delicate origami folds. When they try to run,
    they rip in half.

In this room, light scatters in a prism of all colors.
    Underneath the twinkling fragments
    sits a letter from you.
    I love you. Everything will be okay.
    I am blind.

In this room, there is a boat
    with crisp sails, polished floorboards.
    Just enough room for one. I step in.
    But there is no water and I will wait forever
    in the belly of it.

In this room, I am in your image again.
    Once more unquestioning, a perfect helper.
    We embrace and we mean it.
    This room is not real.

In this room, I was a brief mistake.
   I am placed back in your body — dissolve into you.

In this room, it smells like damp spring.
   Tender saplings line up in rows
   that stretch farther than I can see.
   I stoop to pluck them out from the roots.
   Bunches of limp stems hang from my hands.
      Nothing will ever grow here again.

The most necessary parts of your body
are your palms opening in forgiveness.

Reverse

After Warsan Shire

If I close my eyes hard enough,
    I can take us back. I promise.
   We can go today —
       right now.

Our bodies can fold into themselves
       like origami dolls
    as we become 5
    and 6 again.
  My hair fades into gold wheat,
       your eyes melt into blue puddles,
   and everything becomes okay forever.

I can push his fingers outside of your paper body
    like a birth
    like a death
       but his this time,
     instead of yours.

I can find him. Give him stumps for hands,
      a vacuum where his tongue used to be.

So your skin can be just skin,
   no longer stained the color of those country summers —
grassy and humid and gone.

I'll teach us to tie our own shoelaces.
   I'll walk us both to school.

So you'll be able to stop dreaming of clawing in the dark,
      musky cologne and sticky breath.
   I'll be able to stop hiding in closets,
      praying to the dead.

I can take us to a different home.
   I will break the city in half.
      Scratch everything
      except our hands gripping stuffed animals,
         gripping each other.

If I close my eyes hard enough,
   I can take us back. I promise.
      And in that gold life, that new life,
         there will be so much love
         we won't be able to touch the bottom.

For my best friend, in an undead language

The way you move through the world
makes me think of rain —
taking the shape of anything that will hold you

You are frozen in a moment to me,   forever smoking
on the balcony, staring at the ripened horizon
the golden hour falling   around my hair   your hair damp
from the pool

Webs of mascara dripping   down my cheeks
down my chin   to my knees
we close our eyes, tilt our heads back, and try to build
a time machine in our minds   for a different world
a different tangle of stars   not here, but somewhere else

I would never love you more than this
right here   under our sherbet sun
I still believe if anyone could outrun the past
it would be us   but I could never outrun you

In your last letter   you said
I'm done
sleeping with the doors unlocked,   walking
downtown through alleys with only the moon,
and daring someone to love me like this
                    I do — love you like this

Hope is not a dead language   it whispers in our sleep
do you think we just   forgot how to hear it?

The opposite of gone

I'm not proud of the woman I've become
since

reduced
to a warm spill of alcohol in my stomach
and the base beat of my blood

reduced
to my own thumbs against the hollow of
my throat, instead of yours
as if my cells became you
the moment you left

Pulls of red wine from a mouth
that tastes like yours
with a tongue that
twists your accent of rage

I have become you,   cleaning my blood

I don't belong to myself anymore
The time you twisted my hair
from the root and kicked the air
from my lungs, I think
I swallowed you then
                    I think
there's no separating,
you from me,   me from you
                    I think
for the rest of my life I'll be spitting up blood
I'll be coming up for air
and   instead   choking on your name

What Frida Taught

you are everything. you understand that, right?
you have the entire universe of stars inside your bones,
and you tell me that you don't believe in miracles?
keep walking with your ten toes and ten fingers
and raging heart. you are already whole.
set down your phone. he won't call.
go to a coffee shop and think about God and gravity
and how they must be the same.
Frida taught we are our own unfolding stories,
our own map of the world. you are your own legend.
you loved a man with metal teeth and napalm breath
and it's okay. because it will always be okay.
brush the ashes off your chest and take your
chain-metal heart somewhere else.
you are so goddamn beautiful that you cannot be contained
in a glass jar. you are not a model ship for the world
to look at. you are a lightning bug caught on a July night,
and you would die in there.

The Current Scene of my Childhood Home

The bees are circling something
warm and sweet in the yard.
I was something warm and sweet in the yard
once. The sky was the same color as a slow ache
for years, but now it's blue. Just blue.
Now comes the unfolding of
prairie cones and wild indigos,
dotting color between the trees
as if nothing ever happened here.
I happened here.

In dreams,
my memories are something that can be undone,
like a leaf falling upwards.
As if a flutter of small hands, tender and purposeful,
never struck the sandpaper of a matchbox
again and again underneath the porch until
everything I knew was black dust.
As if I never believed we could have
started new if just given the chance.

But, still, now, a breeze
scented chamomile sweeps through the tall grasses, leaves,
past rabbits drifting to their dens.
It's as if the land itself was healing, slowly forgetting.
I want to heal too. I want to rush back,
put my palms to the earth
and say, "I'm forgiven. I'm forgiven."

It is the nature of grace
to fill empty spaces,
so let yourself be filled.

Barefoot and Running

"You have a second-hand wilderness inside you,"
my great-grandmother warned,
braids sliding down her back
and a cloud of smoke hanging from her lips.

When I think of her, I smell mahogany
and pressed wild flowers inside encyclopedias.
I feel cool mud from kneeling over her in the ground
knowing she was right.

She spit fire and tobacco.
Her voice was a dusty gravel road,
a dream catcher of the stars, the one chord that told me
I could be unconquerable.

Now my heritage is a dead language.
There is no Rosetta Stone
for the unrest written in my bones.
My breath begs questions. I invent words she would say.

"We are not stone women. No. We are soft and earthy,
like clay. They can't break clay.
We curve, twist but can never break."

I can feel her in the texture of my waking dreams
when I am running,
running,   out of breath,   running,
barefoot beneath the pines with white lightning heat
and wet earth caking between my toes.

Across the border of ourselves we, women like wild horses,
will always be barefoot and running.

Found Poem: on notebook paper, torn, in a hotel parking lot off Interstate I-70

I am standing in a field in Breckenridge
thinking about hockey. I close my eyes to see
the smooth glaze of his helmet on the ice and
the sticky shine of my blood
later. He was whiskey breath, whiskey burn,
my whiskey bruises ripening like mumbled curses
beneath the long sleeves of his oversized jersey.
I'd sit alone in my bathtub, with the lukewarm water
rushing down the noisy drain, closing my eyes hard enough
that I couldn't hear a whispering of *bitch love leaving*.
If I'd close my eyes hard enough,
I was never even there at all.

I run my hands through the tips of wild grasses
and remember the rose of my blood blooming
forward and forward, wet petals on the pavement
outside his truck in the 7-Eleven parking lot.
Potholes and winter ice and me.
He would say I slipped
later. The nurses would believe him,
and I would too, just a little.

The wind tangles through my hair,
lifting me up at the edges and I can almost feel
the next morning, soundlessly rolling
out from his heavy arms, so quiet quiet quiet
and staying gone.

> I run my thumbnail down the creases of the paper
> and pocket the poem.
> In this way, I hold space for her.
> In this way, we are never alone.

A letter tucked between the cushions
of a coffee shop couch

Some days you rise in the morning
and your hope doesn't rise with you.

Your bare toes kiss the carpet and it doesn't kiss back.
There's not one silver strand of a story you can tell yourself
that will make it easier
to start this day alone   end this day alone
and spend your moments in-between
quiet, soft, and separate
as if suspended in water
sitting at the bottom of a swimming pool.

There's no help for that.

But the truest thing I know is the light will find you.
Even there.

The bursting and beautiful things meant for you
have been running through the streets to find you
screaming nothing but your name.

Life works like that. You can never be abandoned.

I wish I could take your face between my palms and say:
You wild, infinite thing.
Don't you dare give up.
You are only one small soul but you are so vital.
You're a piece of this shimmering, dancing universe
and we need you here.
We all need you here.

So you can live, even this day,
with your face turned towards the light.

Starling

She was still,   braced against
  the wind in a   snowflake citadel.
    As I watched   the oak nest from
      the ground it was   impossible to tell.
        Then, in one   breath it happened.
        Wind shifted,   wings lifted,
            and she flew
            instead of fell.

Smooth

Black stones
stumble beneath the waves,
tossing and tumbling,
seabed to shore,
hard sharp edges
must be softened
with bursts of chaos

Years of violence and salty rage
will give a velvet texture
to the touch

We are all black stones

14,265 feet

My breath feels sharp
until the peak grows
sharper then the earth
tilts up to meet sky
Clouds press cool against skin
Alpine snow glazes beneath feet
My lips sing psalms of flight
falling off the edge of the world

How is it that my body is empty
and my body is full

pressing hard   against the weight of gravity
being pushed   into valleys and cracks
A storm unravels   slow and strong
I feel thunder   cracking through my ribs,
down my spine, into the softest parts of me
Bolts become a second halo, a burning crown
standing at the height of the world
at the bottom of everything
The polarity,   the storm's energy is shaking awake
a woman I thought I could be but never was
fear forged footsteps instead
I am one story and our stories are all one
struggling   rising
young   unanchored
but enduring and that counts for everything

I turn back to the east
tender pink and gold
and foothold further up up up
the mountain   with the sun

With all your shattered pieces
soldered together,
I've never seen anything so beautiful.

Journey

If I could speak to Grief, I would tell him:

Lying on a boulder next to Clear Creek
with my fingertips submerged in the current,
      know that I am already lost to you.

My aloneness here becomes its own fluency
as I forget everyone that I've ever loved and let disappear,
like a silhouette walking into a fog,
      as I even forget you,
        until your name melts off my tongue for good.

Nothing ever stops leaving. You should know that by now.
And this is where I leave you.

Maybe there is no such thing as forgiveness.
      Maybe all we have is journey
      into places, like silent pine forests
      or fields of columbine,
      where the earth makes up for everything
      we have ever lost.

In these pages I become the leaves all around me
      yellow   orange   red
        ready for a generous forgetting,
        for the gentle fall,

            so someday I can start again.

ACKNOWLEDGMENTS

Thank you to my beloved family and friends for
encouraging me to find my voice
and believing in me always.
Thank you for your unconditional love.
A special thank you goes out to my mom and dad.
I love you so much.

ABOUT THE AUTHOR

Morgan Liphart is a poet and lawyer living in Colorado. Her creative work expresses lyrical reflection on current social issues and her own personal experiences moving from the plains of Illinois to the Mountain West. Her poetry has appeared in anthologies and journals across the United States, such as *The Comstock Review, Magnolia, Bluestem, Chicken Soup for the Soul, Third Wednesday, Front Range Review,* and *Off the Coast.*

You can find Morgan Liphart at morganliphart.com and on Instagram at @mliphart.

If you've enjoyed *Barefoot and Running*, please share on social media or leave a review with your favorite book retailer. Your support for independent authors is appreciated!

CPSIA information can be obtained
at www.ICGtesting.com
Printed in the USA
LVHW051545080321
680847LV00005B/799

9 781735 957906